MAD LIBS®

GRADUATION MAD LIBS

By Roger Price and Leonard Stern

PSS!
PRICE STERN SLOAN

PRICE STERN SLOAN
Published by the Penguin Group
Penguin Group (USA) Inc., 375 Hudson Street, New York, New York 10014, USA
Penguin Group (Canada), 90 Eglinton Avenue East,
Suite 700, Toronto, Ontario M4P 2Y3, Canada
(a division of Pearson Penguin Canada Inc.)
Penguin Books Ltd., 80 Strand, London WC2R 0RL, England
Penguin Group Ireland, 25 St. Stephen's Green, Dublin 2, Ireland
(a division of Penguin Books Ltd.)
Penguin Group (Australia), 250 Camberwell Road, Camberwell,
Victoria 3124, Australia
(a division of Pearson Australia Group Pty. Ltd.)
Penguin Books India Pvt. Ltd., 11 Community Centre, Panchsheel Park,
New Delhi—110 017, India
Penguin Group (NZ), 67 Apollo Drive, Rosedale, Auckland 0632, New Zealand
(a division of Pearson New Zealand Ltd.)
Penguin Books (South Africa) (Pty.) Ltd., 24 Sturdee Avenue,
Rosebank, Johannesburg 2196, South Africa

Penguin Books Ltd., Registered Offices:
80 Strand, London WC2R 0RL, England

Published by Price Stern Sloan,
a division of Penguin Young Readers Group,
345 Hudson Street, New York, New York 10014.

ISBN 978-0-8431-1349-5

12 14 15 13 11

MAD LIBS
INSTRUCTIONS

MAD LIBS® is a game for people who don't like games!
It can be played by one, two, three, four, or forty.

• RIDICULOUSLY SIMPLE DIRECTIONS

In this tablet you will find stories containing blank spaces where words are
left out. One player, the READER, selects one of these stories. The READER
does not tell anyone what the story is about. Instead, he/she asks the other
players, the WRITERS, to give him/her words. These words are used to fill
in the blank spaces in the story.

• TO PLAY

The READER asks each WRITER in turn to call out a word—an adjective or
a noun or whatever the space calls for—and uses them to fill in the blank
spaces in the story. The result is a MAD LIBS® game.

When the READER then reads the completed MAD LIBS® game to the other
players, they will discover that they have written a story that is fantastic,
screamingly funny, shocking, silly, crazy, or just plain dumb—depending
upon which words each WRITER called out.

• EXAMPLE (*Before* and *After*)

" _____ !" he said _____
      EXCLAMATION   ADVERB

as he jumped into his convertible _____ and
                                              NOUN

drove off with his _____ wife.
                       ADJECTIVE

" *Ouch!* !" he said *Stupidly*
      EXCLAMATION   ADVERB

as he jumped into his convertible *Cat* and
                                              NOUN

drove off with his *brave* wife.
                       ADJECTIVE

MAD LIBS®
QUICK REVIEW

In case you have forgotten what adjectives, adverbs, nouns, and verbs are, here is a quick review:

An ADJECTIVE describes something or somebody. *Lumpy, soft, ugly, messy,* and *short* are adjectives.

An ADVERB tells how something is done. It modifies a verb and usually ends in "ly." *Modestly, stupidly, greedily,* and *carefully* are adverbs.

A NOUN is the name of a person, place, or thing. *Sidewalk, umbrella, bridle, bathtub,* and *nose* are nouns.

A VERB is an action word. *Run, pitch, jump,* and *swim* are verbs. Put the verbs in past tense if the directions say PAST TENSE. *Ran, pitched, jumped,* and *swam* are verbs in the past tense.

When we ask for A PLACE, we mean any sort of place: a country or city *(Spain, Cleveland)* or a room *(bathroom, kitchen).*

An EXCLAMATION or SILLY WORD is any sort of funny sound, gasp, grunt, or outcry, like *Wow!, Ouch!, Whomp!, Ick!,* and *Gadzooks!*

When we ask for specific words, like a NUMBER, a COLOR, an ANIMAL, or a PART OF THE BODY, we mean a word that is one of those things, like *seven, blue, horse,* or *head.*

When we ask for a PLURAL, it means more than one. For example, *cat* pluralized is *cats.*

MAD LIBS® is fun to play with friends, but you can also play it by yourself! To begin with, DO NOT look at the story on the page below. Fill in the blanks on this page with the words called for. Then, using the words you have selected, fill in the blank spaces in the story.

Now you've created your own hilarious MAD LIBS® game!

FINAL EXAMS

ADJECTIVE_____

NUMBER _____

VERB _____

NUMBER _____

VERB _____

NOUN _____

OCCUPATION _____

VERB _____

PLURAL NOUN _____

TYPE OF SPORT _____

VERB _____

ROOM _____

VERB _____

PERSON IN ROOM (FEMALE)_____

A PLACE _____

NUMBER _____

VERB _____

ADVERB_____

MAD LIBS

FINAL EXAMS

I'm so nervous about taking my final exams! They're going to be so

_____! Can you believe that I have _____
ADJECTIVE   NUMBER

of them? I'll have to _____ for _____ hours!
VERB   NUMBER

I think I'll _____ my _____ exam, but I'm
VERB   NOUN

afraid that my _____ exam will be really hard. My mom
OCCUPATION

said that I have to _____ every night for the next few
VERB

_____, which means that will be less time I have to
PLURAL NOUN

play _____ and _____ on the phone. And
TYPE OF SPORT   VERB

I doubt I'll have any time to clean my _____ or
ROOM

_____ my laundry. My parents promised they would take
VERB

me and my best friend _____ to _____
PERSON IN ROOM (FEMALE)   A PLACE

if we both get at least a/an _____ on each of our exams.
NUMBER

So I'm going to _____ extra _____!
VERB   ADVERB

MAD LIBS® is fun to play with friends, but you can also play it by yourself! To begin with, DO NOT look at the story on the page below. Fill in the blanks on this page with the words called for. Then, using the words you have selected, fill in the blank spaces in the story.

Now you've created your own hilarious MAD LIBS® game!

PARTY TIME!

ADJECTIVE_____

PLURAL NOUN _____

VERB ENDING IN "ING" _____

PLURAL NOUN _____

CELEBRITY (FEMALE) _____

PERSON IN ROOM (MALE)_____

SILLY WORD_____

VERB _____

TYPE OF FOOD (PLURAL) _____

NOUN _____

SAME TYPE OF FOOD (PLURAL)_____

ADJECTIVE_____

ADJECTIVE_____

TYPE OF SHOE (PLURAL) _____

SOMETHING ALIVE _____

NOUN _____

VERB ENDING IN "ING" _____

NOUN _____

SILLY WORD_____

MAD LIBS
PARTY TIME!

One of the most _____ things about graduating is that my
\hspace{4em} ADJECTIVE

_____ are _____ a huge party! I decided
PLURAL NOUN \hspace{4em} VERB ENDING IN "ING"

to have a backyard barbecue for all of my family and _____.
\hspace{20em} PLURAL NOUN

I've invited my best friends _____, _____,
\hspace{8em} CELEBRITY (FEMALE) \hspace{2em} PERSON IN ROOM (MALE)

and of course my teacher Mrs. _____. My dad is going
\hspace{10em} SILLY WORD

to _____ hamburgers and _____ on his
\hspace{2em} VERB \hspace{8em} TYPE OF FOOD (PLURAL)

shiny new _____. He always thinks his _____
\hspace{4em} NOUN \hspace{10em} SAME TYPE OF FOOD (PLURAL)

taste really _____, but I think they taste like _____
\hspace{6em} ADJECTIVE \hspace{10em} ADJECTIVE

_____. My mom is going to make her famous
TYPE OF SHOE (PLURAL)

_____ salad, which is my favorite _____
SOMETHING ALIVE \hspace{10em} NOUN

ever! Mom said after we finish _____, we can go
\hspace{8em} VERB ENDING IN "ING"

swimming in our new _____. _____!
\hspace{6em} NOUN \hspace{4em} SILLY WORD

From GRADUATION MAD LIBS® • Copyright © 2005 by Price Stern Sloan, a division of
Penguin Young Readers Group, 345 Hudson Street, New York, New York 10014.

MAD LIBS® is fun to play with friends, but you can also play it by yourself! To begin with, DO NOT look at the story on the page below. Fill in the blanks on this page with the words called for. Then, using the words you have selected, fill in the blank spaces in the story.

Now you've created your own hilarious MAD LIBS® game!

GIFTS FOR THE GRAD

EXCLAMATION _____

ADJECTIVE _____

NUMBER _____

PLURAL NOUN _____

NOUN _____

VERB _____

A PLACE _____

PERSON IN ROOM (FEMALE) _____

NOUN _____

SOMETHING ALIVE _____

ADJECTIVE _____

NOUN _____

NOUN _____

A PLACE _____

NOUN _____

LANGUAGE _____

FOREIGN COUNTRY _____

ROOM _____

NOUN _____

VEHICLE _____

CELEBRITY (MALE) _____

COLOR _____

NUMBER _____

MAD LIBS

GIFTS FOR THE GRAD

_____! I got so many _____ graduation
EXCLAMATION   ADJECTIVE

presents! I counted them and can you believe I have _____
                                                    NUMBER

presents in total? That's a lot of _____! My parents got
                                    PLURAL NOUN

me a brand-new _____ so that I can _____
                NOUN   VERB

my homework when I get to _____. My grandma
                            A PLACE

_____ bought me a beautiful _____
PERSON IN ROOM (FEMALE)   NOUN

shaped like a/an _____. It's _____! She said
                  SOMETHING ALIVE   ADJECTIVE

she had one just like it when she was a young _____.
                                               NOUN

My little sister bought me a bright red _____. I can't
                                          NOUN

wait to wear it to _____! My best _____ from
                    A PLACE   NOUN

_____ class bought me a map of _____.
LANGUAGE   FOREIGN COUNTRY

I can't wait to hang it in the _____! But my very
                                ROOM

favorite _____ is the new _____ my
          NOUN   VEHICLE

uncle _____ gave me. It's _____ and
       CELEBRITY (MALE)   COLOR

goes _____ mph!
      NUMBER

MAD LIBS® is fun to play with friends, but you can also play it by yourself! To begin with, DO NOT look at the story on the page below. Fill in the blanks on this page with the words called for. Then, using the words you have selected, fill in the blank spaces in the story.

Now you've created your own hilarious MAD LIBS® game!

CLASS TRIP

SILLY WORD_____

A PLACE _____

VERB _____

COLOR_____

ARTICLE OF CLOTHING_____

PLURAL NOUN _____

NOUN _____

CELEBRITY (FEMALE) _____

VERB ENDING IN "ING" _____

VERB _____

ADJECTIVE_____

SAME SILLY WORD _____

NOUN _____

VERB (PAST TENSE)_____

SAME SILLY WORD _____

ADJECTIVE_____

SAME PLACE _____

PLURAL NOUN _____

VERB _____

VEHICLE (PLURAL) _____

ADJECTIVE_____

PLURAL NOUN _____

MAD LIBS®

CLASS TRIP

For our final class trip our teacher Mr. _____ announced

SILLY WORD

that we're going to _____! I'm so excited I can hardly

A PLACE

_____! I'm bringing my new _____

VERB _____ COLOR

_____, my fancy _____, and of course

ARTICLE OF CLOTHING _____ PLURAL NOUN

my _____. My best friend _____ is

NOUN _____ CELEBRITY (FEMALE)

_____ too, which will _____ the trip

VERB ENDING IN "ING" _____ VERB

even more _____. Mr. _____ said we can

ADJECTIVE _____ SAME SILLY WORD

even share a/an _____! When I heard, I was so excited

NOUN

I _____! Mr. _____ said that while we're

VERB (PAST TENSE) _____ SAME SILLY WORD

visiting the _____ village of _____ we can

ADJECTIVE _____ SAME PLACE

do everything that the _____ do. We'll be able to

PLURAL NOUN

_____ in huge _____ and sleep in

VERB _____ VEHICLE (PLURAL)

_____ _____.

ADJECTIVE _____ PLURAL NOUN

From GRADUATION MAD LIBS® • Copyright © 2005 by Price Stern Sloan, a division of
Penguin Young Readers Group, 345 Hudson Street, New York, New York 10014.

MAD LIBS® is fun to play with friends, but you can also play it by yourself! To begin with, DO NOT look at the story on the page below. Fill in the blanks on this page with the words called for. Then, using the words you have selected, fill in the blank spaces in the story.

Now you've created your own hilarious MAD LIBS® game!

YOU'RE INVITED!

ADJECTIVE_____

VERB ENDING IN "ING" _____

TYPE OF FOOD (PLURAL) _____

TYPE OF LIQUID _____

ADJECTIVE_____

VERB _____

ARTICLE OF CLOTHING_____

ADJECTIVE_____

PART OF THE BODY (PLURAL) _____

VERB ENDING IN "ING" _____

PERSON IN ROOM (MALE)_____

VERB ENDING IN "ING" _____

SOMETHING ALIVE _____

PLURAL NOUN _____

CELEBRITY (FEMALE) _____

ARTICLE OF CLOTHING (PLURAL)_____

MAD LIBS®

YOU'RE INVITED!

Here are some _____ tips for _____ the
                    ADJECTIVE   VERB ENDING IN "ING"

best graduation party ever!

- Provide your guests with plenty of _____
                                      TYPE OF FOOD (PLURAL)

  and _____. No one likes to be hungry
        TYPE OF LIQUID

  or _____!
       ADJECTIVE

- _____ your fanciest _____
       VERB   ARTICLE OF CLOTHING

  and wear _____ shoes. You wouldn't want your
             ADJECTIVE

  _____ to hurt while you're
  PART OF THE BODY (PLURAL)

  _____ with _____.
  VERB ENDING IN "ING"   PERSON IN ROOM (MALE)

- When _____ at a party, it's always polite
          VERB ENDING IN "ING"

  to bring fresh _____ or a box of
                   SOMETHING ALIVE

  _____. At least that's what _____
  PLURAL NOUN   CELEBRITY (FEMALE)

  says you should do!

- Last but not least, you should always wear clean

  _____!
  ARTICLE OF CLOTHING (PLURAL)

MAD LIBS® is fun to play with friends, but you can also play it by yourself! To begin with, DO NOT look at the story on the page below. Fill in the blanks on this page with the words called for. Then, using the words you have selected, fill in the blank spaces in the story.

Now you've created your own hilarious MAD LIBS® game!

FRIENDSHIPS

ADJECTIVE _____

ADJECTIVE _____

ADJECTIVE _____

PLURAL NOUN _____

ADJECTIVE _____

NOUN _____

PLURAL NOUN _____

LAST NAME OF PERSON IN ROOM _____

NOUN _____

PLURAL NOUN _____

CELEBRITY (MALE) _____

PLURAL NOUN _____

NOUN _____

NOUN _____

PERSON IN ROOM _____

NOUN _____

NOUN _____

NOUN _____

ADJECTIVE _____

PLURAL NOUN _____

NOUN _____

MAD LIBS
FRIENDSHIPS

One of the particularly _____ things about graduating is
                                     ADJECTIVE

the _____ friendships that you make. There's a/an
       ADJECTIVE

_____ saying that the _____ that begin
ADJECTIVE   PLURAL NOUN

in _____ school often last a lifetime. A shining
      ADJECTIVE

_____ of this is my own father's relationship with three
NOUN

_____. One of them, Ralph _____,
PLURAL NOUN   LAST NAME OF PERSON IN ROOM

is a fashion _____ who designs women's _____.
           NOUN   PLURAL NOUN

_____, who is six feet nine _____ tall, is a
CELEBRITY (MALE)   PLURAL NOUN

professional _____ player, and Dad's oldest _____ is
         NOUN   NOUN

_____, who sells cars and _____
PERSON IN ROOM   NOUN

insurance. They meet regularly at a coffee _____ in our
                                NOUN

_____ and talk about _____ times. I hope my
NOUN   ADJECTIVE

best _____ will be part of my _____ as long as
    PLURAL NOUN   NOUN

my dad's friends have been in his.

MAD LIBS® is fun to play with friends, but you can also play it by yourself! To begin with, DO NOT look at the story on the page below. Fill in the blanks on this page with the words called for. Then, using the words you have selected, fill in the blank spaces in the story.

Now you've created your own hilarious MAD LIBS® game!

CLASS PRESIDENT

PLURAL NOUN _____

VERB _____

PLURAL NOUN _____

YEAR _____

VERB (PAST TENSE) _____

NUMBER _____

LANGUAGE _____

PLURAL NOUN _____

FOREIGN COUNTRY _____

NUMBER _____

ADJECTIVE _____

SILLY WORD _____

NUMBER _____

ADJECTIVE _____

OCCUPATION (PLURAL) _____

ADJECTIVE _____

VERB ENDING IN "ING" _____

SAME YEAR _____

ADJECTIVE _____

MAD LIBS
CLASS PRESIDENT

Good morning, ladies and _____. As your class president,
                              PLURAL NOUN

I'd like to _____ a few _____ about the
               VERB   PLURAL NOUN

graduating class of _____. We've all _____
                          YEAR   VERB (PAST TENSE)

hard over the past _____ years and what a great time
                         NUMBER

we've had! We've studied _____, learned about
                              LANGUAGE

_____ in _____, and even learned how
  PLURAL NOUN   FOREIGN COUNTRY

to count to _____! That's pretty _____ if
                 NUMBER   ADJECTIVE

you ask me. Especially since we had Mrs. _____ as our
                                              SILLY WORD

teacher for the past _____ years. She was one of the most
                          NUMBER

_____ _____ we've ever had! I think
  ADJECTIVE   OCCUPATION (PLURAL)

this year's class is the most _____ ever. Although I'm
                                  ADJECTIVE

sad to be _____, I know the class of _____
             VERB ENDING IN "ING"   SAME YEAR

will do _____ things in the future.
           ADJECTIVE

From GRADUATION MAD LIBS® • Copyright © 2005 by Price Stern Sloan, a division of
Penguin Young Readers Group, 345 Hudson Street, New York, New York 10014.

MAD LIBS® is fun to play with friends, but you can also play it by yourself! To begin with, DO NOT look at the story on the page below. Fill in the blanks on this page with the words called for. Then, using the words you have selected, fill in the blank spaces in the story.

Now you've created your own hilarious MAD LIBS® game!

OUR YEARBOOK

ADJECTIVE_____

EXCLAMATION_____

VERB (PAST TENSE)_____

VERB (PAST TENSE)_____

ADJECTIVE_____

TYPE OF SPORT _____

SILLY WORD_____

LANGUAGE _____

PLURAL NOUN _____

NUMBER _____

PERSON IN ROOM (MALE)_____

PERSON IN ROOM (FEMALE)_____

OCCUPATION _____

ADJECTIVE_____

OCCUPATION (PLURAL) _____

VERB ENDING IN "ING" _____

PLURAL NOUN _____

VERB _____

PLURAL NOUN _____

PART OF THE BODY_____

MAD LIBS®
OUR YEARBOOK

On the last day of school, our _____ yearbooks came
_____ ADJECTIVE

out. Everyone yelled _____ and _____ to
_____ EXCLAMATION _____ VERB (PAST TENSE)

grab one. When we _____ it, we couldn't believe how
_____ VERB (PAST TENSE)

_____ it came out! It was filled with pictures of our
ADJECTIVE

_____ team the _____, the _____
TYPE OF SPORT _____ SILLY WORD _____ LANGUAGE

club, and our school marching band the _____. There
_____ PLURAL NOUN

were _____ pages devoted to Homecoming, where
_____ NUMBER

_____ and _____ were named king
PERSON IN ROOM (MALE) _____ PERSON IN ROOM (FEMALE)

and _____. There were even snapshots of our
_____ OCCUPATION

_____ _____. After we finished
ADJECTIVE _____ OCCUPATION (PLURAL)

_____ through all of the cool _____,
VERB ENDING IN "ING" _____ PLURAL NOUN

everyone grabbed a pen so we could _____ onc
_____ VERB

another's books. I signed so many _____, I thought my
_____ PLURAL NOUN

_____ would fall off!
PART OF THE BODY

From GRADUATION MAD LIBS® • Copyright © 2005 by Price Stern Sloan, a division of
Penguin Young Readers Group, 345 Hudson Street, New York, New York 10014.

MAD LIBS® is fun to play with friends, but you can also play it by yourself! To begin with, DO NOT look at the story on the page below. Fill in the blanks on this page with the words called for. Then, using the words you have selected, fill in the blank spaces in the story.

Now you've created your own hilarious MAD LIBS® game!

WHEN I GROW UP

NUMBER _____

VERB ENDING IN "ING" _____

NOUN _____

LAST NAME OF PERSON IN ROOM_____

VERB ENDING IN "ING" _____

ADVERB_____

OCCUPATION _____

OCCUPATION _____

ADJECTIVE_____

NUMBER _____

A PLACE _____

PLURAL NOUN _____

NUMBER _____

NOUN _____

A PLACE _____

PLURAL NOUN _____

VEHICLE _____

ADJECTIVE_____

VERB ENDING IN "ING" _____

MAD LIBS
WHEN I GROW UP

Now that I've graduated from grade _____, I'm going to

NUMBER

start _____ more often. After all, I'm practically

VERB ENDING IN "ING"

a/an _____! Since I want to be just like Donald

NOUN

_____ when I grow up, I'd better start

LAST NAME OF PERSON IN ROOM

_____ as _____ as possible. I think this

VERB ENDING IN "ING"   ADVERB

summer I'm going to get a part-time job as a/an _____ or

OCCUPATION

a/an _____.That will teach me how to be _____

OCCUPATION   ADJECTIVE

and maybe I'll even make _____ dollars! Then I can put all

NUMBER

of my money in the _____ and collect _____.

A PLACE   PLURAL NOUN

When I retire at age _____, I'll be a/an _____.

NUMBER   NOUN

Maybe I'll even get to live on the beach in _____, buy

A PLACE

expensive _____, and drive a fancy _____.

PLURAL NOUN   VEHICLE

Wouldn't that be _____? I'd better start

ADJECTIVE

_____ right away!

VERB ENDING IN "ING"

From GRADUATION MAD LIBS® • Copyright © 2005 by Price Stern Sloan, a division of
Penguin Young Readers Group, 345 Hudson Street, New York, New York 10014.

MAD LIBS® is fun to play with friends, but you can also play it by yourself! To begin with, DO NOT look at the story on the page below. Fill in the blanks on this page with the words called for. Then, using the words you have selected, fill in the blank spaces in the story.

Now you've created your own hilarious MAD LIBS® game!

THANK YOU

PLURAL NOUN _____

A PLACE _____

ADVERB _____

NOUN _____

VERB _____

NUMBER _____

LANGUAGE _____

ADJECTIVE _____

PLURAL NOUN _____

CELEBRITY (FEMALE) _____

VERB _____

PERSON IN ROOM (FEMALE) _____

CELEBRITY (MALE) _____

PART OF THE BODY _____

VERB ENDING IN "ING" _____

ROOM _____

VERB ENDING IN "ING" _____

A PLACE _____

NOUN _____

NOUN _____

SILLY WORD _____

NOUN _____

MAD LIBS®
THANK YOU

There are so many _____ I want to thank for helping
                PLURAL NOUN

me graduate from _____. First of all, I have to thank my
               A PLACE

mom and dad. They've _____ helped me with my
              ADVERB

_____, taught me how to _____ to
    NOUN   VERB

_____, and how to write in _____. They're
    NUMBER   LANGUAGE

the most _____ _____ ever! Next I'd like to
      ADJECTIVE   PLURAL NOUN

thank my teacher _____ for always showing me how to
            CELEBRITY (FEMALE)

properly _____ my ABCs and 123s. Of course I have to thank
      VERB

my best friends, _____ and _____.
      PERSON IN ROOM (FEMALE)   CELEBRITY (MALE)

I will always hold close to my _____ the times we spent
               PART OF THE BODY

_____ in my _____ and _____ in
VERB ENDING IN "ING"   ROOM   VERB ENDING IN "ING"

the _____. I would like to give a special thank-you to Mrs.
    A PLACE

_____, who taught me how to play the _____.
    NOUN   NOUN

And thank you, Mr. _____! Without you, I never would
            SILLY WORD

have passed _____ class!
      NOUN

MAD LIBS® is fun to play with friends, but you can also play it by yourself! To begin with, DO NOT look at the story on the page below. Fill in the blanks on this page with the words called for. Then, using the words you have selected, fill in the blank spaces in the story.

Now you've created your own hilarious MAD LIBS® game!

TIPS FOR THE NEW GRAD

A PLACE _____

PLURAL NOUN _____

VERB _____

NOUN _____

NOUN _____

ADJECTIVE _____

CELEBRITY (MALE) _____

ARTICLE OF CLOTHING _____

ADJECTIVE _____

PLURAL NOUN _____

NOUN _____

OCCUPATION _____

NUMBER _____

NOUN _____

MAD LIBS
TIPS FOR THE NEW GRAD

Now that you've finally graduated from _____, you'll
A PLACE

need some really good _____ to make sure you
PLURAL NOUN

_____ your way to the top! The following tips will help
VERB

you become a huge _____:
NOUN

• Carry a/an _____ with you at all times. This
NOUN

   will make you look very _____. People
ADJECTIVE

   will think you look just like _____.
CELEBRITY (MALE)

• Always wear a clean, pressed _____. After all,
ARTICLE OF CLOTHING

   nobody will hire a/an _____ dresser!
ADJECTIVE

• It's a smart idea to have your own customized

   _____. That way, people will always
PLURAL NOUN

   remember your name and phone _____.
NOUN

• Be sure you visit the _____ at least
OCCUPATION

   _____ times a week. You wouldn't want
NUMBER

   your _____ to look out of place!
NOUN

MAD LIBS® is fun to play with friends, but you can also play it by yourself! To begin with, DO NOT look at the story on the page below. Fill in the blanks on this page with the words called for. Then, using the words you have selected, fill in the blank spaces in the story.

Now you've created your own hilarious MAD LIBS® game!

FINAL FAREWELL

A PLACE _____

ADJECTIVE _____

OCCUPATION (PLURAL) _____

PLURAL NOUN _____

NOUN _____

PLURAL NOUN _____

SILLY WORD_____

TYPE OF FOOD_____

TYPE OF FOOD_____

NOUN _____

PERSON IN ROOM (FEMALE)_____

NOUN _____

PERSON IN ROOM (MALE)_____

NOUN _____

ADVERB_____

SILLY WORD_____

ADJECTIVE_____

VERB (PAST TENSE)_____

PART OF THE BODY _____

VERB ENDING IN "ING" _____

MAD LIBS®
FINAL FAREWELL

My last day at _____ was extremely _____.
_____A PLACE_____ _____ADJECTIVE_____

First, our _____ told us how proud they were that
_____OCCUPATION (PLURAL)_____

we turned into such great _____. Then we had a/an
_____PLURAL NOUN_____

_____ where all of our family and _____
_____NOUN_____ _____PLURAL NOUN_____

came to bid us farewell. Mrs. _____ surprised us with a
_____SILLY WORD_____

big _____ with _____ frosting! I thought it
_____TYPE OF FOOD_____ _____TYPE OF FOOD_____

tasted like a/an _____, but my friend _____
_____NOUN_____ _____PERSON IN ROOM (FEMALE)_____

thought it was the best piece of _____ she ever had!
_____NOUN_____

Then Mr. _____ announced that he had a big
_____PERSON IN ROOM (MALE)_____

_____ for us! _____, my favorite band
_____NOUN_____ _____ADVERB_____

_____ arrived! They were _____! They
_____SILLY WORD_____ _____ADJECTIVE_____

_____ all of my favorite songs like "Rock Your
_____VERB (PAST TENSE)_____

_____" and "We're _____"! This was
_____PART OF THE BODY_____ _____VERB ENDING IN "ING"_____

the coolest graduation ever!

MAD LIBS® is fun to play with friends, but you can also play it by yourself! To begin with, DO NOT look at the story on the page below. Fill in the blanks on this page with the words called for. Then, using the words you have selected, fill in the blank spaces in the story.

Now you've created your own hilarious MAD LIBS® game!

MY FIRST GRADUATION

NUMBER _____

PART OF THE BODY_____

ADJECTIVE_____

PLURAL NOUN _____

ADJECTIVE_____

VERB _____

PLURAL NOUN _____

NOUN _____

PLURAL NOUN _____

PLURAL NOUN _____

LIQUID_____

ADJECTIVE_____

NOUN _____

NOUN _____

NOUN _____

ADJECTIVE_____

NOUN _____

NOUN _____

MAD LIBS

MY FIRST GRADUATION

Even though _____ years have gone by, my kindergarten
            NUMBER

graduation is still fresh in my _____. I have _____
                                PART OF THE BODY   ADJECTIVE

memories of my very first day. I remember walking into the room

with my _____ shaking. Fortunately, the teacher was very
        PLURAL NOUN

_____ and made me _____. In no time at all, I
   ADJECTIVE   VERB

learned how to count _____, write my own full
                        PLURAL NOUN

_____, and color _____. Every day, we had snack
    NOUN   PLURAL NOUN

time. Some of us ate cheese and _____, others had cookies
                                   PLURAL NOUN

and _____. The rest of the day, the teacher read a/an
       LIQUID

_____ _____ to us, like *Charlie and the*
   ADJECTIVE   NOUN

_____ *Factory*. All of my days in kindergarten are etched
    NOUN

in my _____. I really hated to leave. Actually, I didn't
         NOUN

graduate! The nurse sent me home that day because I had a/an

_____ cold and a hacking _____. The school
   ADJECTIVE   NOUN

eventually mailed my _____ to me.
                        NOUN

From GRADUATION MAD LIBS® • Copyright © 2005 by Price Stern Sloan, a division of
Penguin Young Readers Group, 345 Hudson Street, New York, New York 10014.

MAD LIBS® is fun to play with friends, but you can also play it by yourself! To begin with, DO NOT look at the story on the page below. Fill in the blanks on this page with the words called for. Then, using the words you have selected, fill in the blank spaces in the story.

Now you've created your own hilarious MAD LIBS® game!

MOST LIKELY TO...

NUMBER _____

VERB _____

PERSON IN ROOM (FEMALE)_____

VERB _____

A PLACE _____

NOUN _____

SILLY WORD_____

ADJECTIVE_____

VERB _____

PERSON IN ROOM (FEMALE)_____

A PLACE _____

NUMBER _____

LANGUAGE _____

SILLY WORD_____

OCCUPATION _____

VERB _____

VERB _____

ADJECTIVE_____

A PLACE _____

VERB ENDING IN "ING" _____

PLURAL NOUN _____

MAD LIBS®
MOST LIKELY TO . . .

_____ pages of our yearbook were dedicated to "The Person
NUMBER

Most Likely To . . ." when we _____ up. My best friend,
VERB

_____, was voted most likely to _____
PERSON IN ROOM (FEMALE)   VERB

in _____, because she wants to be a movie _____
A PLACE   NOUN

when she grows up. Peter _____ was voted most
SILLY WORD

_____, because all the girls in my class _____
ADJECTIVE   VERB

when he walks by. _____ was voted most likely
PERSON IN ROOM (FEMALE)

to graduate from _____ with honors, because she got
A PLACE

a/an _____ on every _____ test last
NUMBER   LANGUAGE

semester. My friend _____ got everyone's vote for the
SILLY WORD

girl most likely to be a/an _____, because she loves to
OCCUPATION

make people _____. And me? I was named the most likely
VERB

to _____, because of all of my _____
VERB   ADJECTIVE

adventures traveling to _____ and _____
A PLACE   VERB ENDING IN "ING"

through the Rocky _____.
PLURAL NOUN

From GRADUATION MAD LIBS® • Copyright © 2005 by Price Stern Sloan, a division of
Penguin Young Readers Group, 345 Hudson Street, New York, New York 10014.

MAD LIBS® is fun to play with friends, but you can also play it by yourself! To begin with, DO NOT look at the story on the page below. Fill in the blanks on this page with the words called for. Then, using the words you have selected, fill in the blank spaces in the story.

Now you've created your own hilarious MAD LIBS® gamc!

MEMORIES

ADJECTIVE_____

ADJECTIVE_____

ADJECTIVE_____

ADJECTIVE_____

PLURAL NOUN _____

VERB ENDING IN "ING" _____

PLURAL NOUN _____

VERB ENDING IN "ING" _____

PLURAL NOUN _____

NOUN _____

ADJECTIVE_____

NOUN _____

ADJECTIVE_____

PLURAL NOUN _____

PLURAL NOUN _____

PLURAL NOUN _____

ADJECTIVE_____

PLURAL NOUN _____

MAD LIBS®
MEMORIES

Some of the _____ memories I have of _____
ADJECTIVE   ADJECTIVE

school concern the _____ trips we took to so many
ADJECTIVE

_____ places. I'll always remember a visit to the zoo where
ADJECTIVE

we saw the wild _____ _____ in their cages
PLURAL NOUN   VERB ENDING IN "ING"

and the flying _____ practically _____ in
PLURAL NOUN   VERB ENDING IN "ING"

everyone's hair. There were also the wonderful science

_____ at the _____ museum and the trips to a/an
PLURAL NOUN   NOUN

_____ theater where we saw *The Lion* _____ and
ADJECTIVE   NOUN

The _____ *Mermaid.* These are the kinds of _____
ADJECTIVE   PLURAL NOUN

that will last forever. I'm sure I'll be telling my own _____
PLURAL NOUN

about them in _____ to come and, hopefully, they'll be
PLURAL NOUN

visiting _____ places and creating _____ of
ADJECTIVE   PLURAL NOUN

their own.

From GRADUATION MAD LIBS® • Copyright © 2005 by Price Stern Sloan, a division of
Penguin Young Readers Group, 345 Hudson Street, New York, New York 10014.

MAD LIBS® is fun to play with friends, but you can also play it by yourself! To begin with, DO NOT look at the story on the page below. Fill in the blanks on this page with the words called for. Then, using the words you have selected, fill in the blank spaces in the story.

Now you've created your own hilarious MAD LIBS® game!

MY DIPLOMA

ADJECTIVE_____

ADJECTIVE_____

COLOR_____

PLURAL NOUN _____

ADJECTIVE_____

SILLY WORD_____

NOUN _____

VERB _____

EXCLAMATION_____

VERB (PAST TENSE)_____

ADJECTIVE_____

VERB ENDING IN "ING" _____

VERB _____

ADJECTIVE_____

PERSON IN ROOM (MALE)_____

VERB _____

ADVERB_____

COLOR_____

VERB _____

ADVERB_____

NOUN _____

ROOM _____

MAD LIBS

MY DIPLOMA

I can't believe I got my _____ diploma! It's
                            ADJECTIVE

_____! It is _____ and lists all of the
ADJECTIVE   COLOR

_____ I took during _____ school.
PLURAL NOUN   ADJECTIVE

When Principal _____ called my _____
                 SILLY WORD   NOUN

to _____ up and get it, I was so excited I yelled
    VERB

_____! I practically _____ it out of his hand!
EXCLAMATION   VERB (PAST TENSE)

My parents were so _____ to see me _____
                     ADJECTIVE   VERB ENDING IN "ING"

my diploma that they actually started to _____! My
                                            VERB

_____ little brother _____ started to
ADJECTIVE   PERSON IN ROOM (MALE)

_____ so _____ that my mom's face turned
VERB   ADVERB

bright _____, which made her _____ even
        COLOR   VERB

more. When I got home, I _____ put my diploma in a/an
                          ADVERB

_____ and hung it up in the _____.
NOUN   ROOM

MAD LIBS® is fun to play with friends, but you can also play it by yourself! To begin with, DO NOT look at the story on the page below. Fill in the blanks on this page with the words called for. Then, using the words you have selected, fill in the blank spaces in the story.

Now you've created your own hilarious MAD LIBS® game!

MY TEACHERS

PLURAL NOUN _____

A PLACE _____

ADJECTIVE_____

SILLY WORD_____

VERB _____

NOUN _____

NUMBER _____

PERSON IN ROOM (FEMALE)_____

TYPE OF FOOD (PLURAL) _____

LANGUAGE _____

CELEBRITY (MALE)_____

OCCUPATION (PLURAL) _____

NOUN _____

PLURAL NOUN _____

VERB _____

PLURAL NOUN _____

ADJECTIVE_____

ADVERB_____

LAST NAME OF PERSON _____

NUMBER _____

NOUN _____

ADVERB_____

SAME LAST NAME OF PERSON_____

MAD LIBS

MY TEACHERS

One of the _____ I will miss most about graduating
         PLURAL NOUN

from _____ is all of the _____ teachers
         A PLACE   ADJECTIVE

that I had. There is Mr. _____, who taught me how to
                              SILLY WORD

_____ the _____ and count to _____.
      VERB   NOUN   NUMBER

Then there is Mrs. _____, who always brought
                        PERSON IN ROOM (FEMALE)

_____ to _____ class. And _____
TYPE OF FOOD (PLURAL)   LANGUAGE   CELEBRITY (MALE)

is one of my favorite _____ ever! He was the school's
                          OCCUPATION (PLURAL)

drama _____, and he put on the best _____ ever!
            NOUN   PLURAL NOUN

He let me _____ the lead in the school play *Guys and*
                VERB

_____. But I think out of all my _____ teachers,
PLURAL NOUN   ADJECTIVE

the one I will miss _____ is Mrs. _____.
                        ADVERB   LAST NAME OF PERSON

She always gave me a/an _____ on _____ tests and
                              NUMBER   NOUN

would _____ help me with my homework. I'll miss you,
            ADVERB

Mrs. _____!
      SAME LAST NAME OF PERSON

From GRADUATION MAD LIBS® • Copyright © 2005 by Price Stern Sloan, a division of
Penguin Young Readers Group, 345 Hudson Street, New York, New York 10014.

MAD LIBS® is fun to play with friends, but you can also play it by yourself! To begin with, DO NOT look at the story on the page below. Fill in the blanks on this page with the words called for. Then, using the words you have selected, fill in the blank spaces in the story.

Now you've created your own hilarious MAD LIBS® game!

THE FAREWELL DANCE

ADJECTIVE_____

PLURAL NOUN _____

PLURAL NOUN _____

ADJECTIVE_____

NOUN _____

ADJECTIVE_____

ADJECTIVE_____

PLURAL NOUN _____

NOUN _____

ADVERB_____

ADJECTIVE_____

PLURAL NOUN _____

PLURAL NOUN _____

NOUN _____

PLURAL NOUN _____

NOUN _____

MAD LIBS

THE FAREWELL DANCE

A farewell dance is both a happy and a/an _____

    ADJECTIVE

occasion. It may be the last time you see many of your

_____ with whom you've spent the most important

    PLURAL NOUN

_____ of your life. This year our _____

    PLURAL NOUN   ADJECTIVE

dance will be held in the school _____. It will be

                                         NOUN

decorated in a very _____ fashion. On the walls will

                              ADJECTIVE

be caricatures of our _____ teachers. Helium

                                   ADJECTIVE

_____ will be floating overhead, and a revolving crystal

    PLURAL NOUN

_____ will _____ reflect light on the

    NOUN   ADVERB

_____ floor. Most of the boys will be wearing rented

    ADJECTIVE

_____ and most of the girls will be dressed in formal

    PLURAL NOUN

_____. And here's the big surprise: We have enough

    PLURAL NOUN

_____ in our budget to book the Beastie

    NOUN

_____ to supply the music! All in all, it promises to be

    PLURAL NOUN

a/an _____ to remember.

        NOUN

From GRADUATION MAD LIBS® • Copyright © 2005 by Price Stern Sloan, a division of
Penguin Young Readers Group, 345 Hudson Street, New York, New York 10014.

MAD LIBS® is fun to play with friends, but you can also play it by yourself! To begin with, DO NOT look at the story on the page below. Fill in the blanks on this page with the words called for. Then, using the words you have selected, fill in the blank spaces in the story.

Now you've created your own hilarious MAD LIBS® game!

SAYING GOOD-BYE

VERB ENDING IN "ING" _____

PLURAL NOUN _____

VERB _____

CELEBRITY (MALE) _____

NUMBER _____

ADJECTIVE _____

PERSON IN ROOM (FEMALE) _____

TYPE OF SPORT _____

SILLY WORD _____

PLURAL NOUN _____

VERB _____

ADJECTIVE _____

PLURAL NOUN _____

NOUN _____

CELEBRITY (FEMALE) _____

ADVERB _____

TOWN _____

VERB _____

MAD LIBS

SAYING GOOD-BYE

One of the hardest things about _____ from school
                                    VERB ENDING IN "ING"

is saying good-bye to all of my good _____. I'm going to
                                        PLURAL NOUN

_____ them so much! How can I say farewell to my best
    VERB

friend, _____? We've gone to school together since
            CELEBRITY (MALE)

I was _____ years old! Then there is my _____
          NUMBER   ADJECTIVE

friend _____, who was on my _____
        PERSON IN ROOM (FEMALE)   TYPE OF SPORT

team. I'll hate to say _____ to her! Then there's the
                            SILLY WORD

group of _____ that I used to _____ with—they
            PLURAL NOUN   VERB

are the most _____ _____ ever! I'll
                ADJECTIVE   PLURAL NOUN

miss my _____ friend _____ most
            NOUN   CELEBRITY (FEMALE)

_____. But she lives in _____ so I'll get to
    ADVERB   TOWN

_____ her all the time.
    VERB

From GRADUATION MAD LIBS® • Copyright © 2005 by Price Stern Sloan, a division of
Penguin Young Readers Group, 345 Hudson Street, New York, New York 10014.

MAD LIBS® is fun to play with friends, but you can also play it by yourself! To begin with, DO NOT look at the story on the page below. Fill in the blanks on this page with the words called for. Then, using the words you have selected, fill in the blank spaces in the story.

Now you've created your own hilarious MAD LIBS® game!

NEW SCHOOL JITTERS

VERB ENDING IN "ING" _____

NUMBER _____

ADJECTIVE _____

TOWN _____

PLURAL NOUN _____

VEHICLE _____

ADJECTIVE _____

ADJECTIVE _____

PLURAL NOUN _____

VERB ENDING IN "ING" _____

A PLACE _____

TYPE OF SPORT _____

CELEBRITY (MALE) _____

OCCUPATION _____

EXCLAMATION _____

MAD LIBS
NEW SCHOOL JITTERS

Even though I'm not _____ to my new school for
_____ VERB ENDING IN "ING"

another _____ months, I'm already getting _____
_____ NUMBER _____ ADJECTIVE

about it. It's all the way in _____, which is far away from
_____ TOWN

all of my neighborhood _____. Because it's so far away,
_____ PLURAL NOUN

I'll have to take a/an _____ to school. Isn't that
_____ VEHICLE

_____? But even though there are many _____
ADJECTIVE _____ ADJECTIVE

things about starting a new school, there are also lots of things to be

excited about. I can't wait to make new _____, take
_____ PLURAL NOUN

exciting classes like _____, have lunch in the
_____ VERB ENDING IN "ING"

_____, and join the _____ team. Plus, I
A PLACE _____ TYPE OF SPORT

heard that _____ is a/an _____ there!
_____ CELEBRITY (MALE) _____ OCCUPATION

_____! I can't wait for school to start!
EXCLAMATION

MAD LIBS® is fun to play with friends, but you can also play it by yourself! To begin with, DO NOT look at the story on the page below. Fill in the blanks on this page with the words called for. Then, using the words you have selected, fill in the blank spaces in the story.

Now you've created your own hilarious MAD LIBS® game!

CLASS RING

VERB ENDING IN "ING" _____

FOREIGN COUNTRY _____

ADJECTIVE _____

COLOR _____

COLOR _____

COLOR _____

PART OF THE BODY (PLURAL) _____

PERSON IN ROOM (FEMALE) _____

COLOR _____

TYPE OF FOOD _____

CELEBRITY (FEMALE) _____

CELEBRITY (MALE) _____

ADJECTIVE _____

PLURAL NOUN _____

YEAR _____

VERB _____

VERB _____

VERB _____

ROOM _____

ADJECTIVE _____

VERB _____

ADJECTIVE _____

PART OF THE BODY (PLURAL) _____

MAD☺LIBS
CLASS RING

Today we're _____ our class rings! They came all the
VERB ENDING IN "ING"

way from _____ and are _____ colors like
FOREIGN COUNTRY   ADJECTIVE

_____ and _____. My ring is bright _____
COLOR   COLOR   COLOR

and matches my _____ perfectly. My best
PART OF THE BODY (PLURAL)

friend _____ picked a/an _____ ring
PERSON IN ROOM (FEMALE)   COLOR

the color of _____. She said it reminds her of the ring
TYPE OF FOOD

that _____ got from _____, even though it's
CELEBRITY (FEMALE)   CELEBRITY (MALE)

not as _____. And guess what? The ring even has our very
ADJECTIVE

own _____ on it and says the "Class of _____"!
PLURAL NOUN   YEAR

I know I'll _____ my class ring for as long as I _____.
VERB   VERB

I am going to _____ it every day and keep it safe in my
VERB

_____. That way my _____ little brother
ROOM   ADJECTIVE

won't be able to _____ his _____ little
VERB   ADJECTIVE

_____ on it!
PART OF THE BODY (PLURAL)

This book is published by

PSS!

PRICE STERN SLOAN

whose other splendid titles include
such literary classics as

Ad Lib Mad Libs®

Best of Mad Libs®

Camp Daze Mad Libs®

Christmas Carol Mad Libs®

Christmas Fun Mad Libs®

Cool Mad Libs®

Dance Mania Mad Libs®

Dear Valentine Letters Mad Libs®

Dinosaur Mad Libs®

Diva Girl Mad Libs®

Dude, Where's My Mad Libs®

Family Tree Mad Libs®

Fun in the Sun Mad Libs®

Girls Just Wanna Have Mad Libs®

Goofy Mad Libs®

Grab Bag Mad Libs®

Graduation Mad Libs®

Grand Slam Mad Libs®

Happily Ever Mad Libs®

Happy Birthday Mad Libs®

Haunted Mad Libs®

Holly, Jolly Mad Libs®

Kid Libs Mad Libs®

Letters From Camp Mad Libs®

Letters to Mom & Dad Mad Libs®

Mad About Animals Mad Libs®

Mad Libs® for President

Mad Libs® from Outer Space

Mad Libs® in Love

Mad Libs® on the Road

Mad Mad Mad Mad Mad Libs®

Monster Mad Libs®

More Best of Mad Libs®

Night of the Living Mad Libs®

Ninjas Mad Libs®

Off-the-Wall Mad Libs®

The Original #1 Mad Libs®

P. S. I Love Mad Libs®

Peace, Love, and Mad Libs®

Pirates Mad Libs®

Prime-Time Mad Libs®

Rock 'n' Roll Mad Libs®

Slam Dunk Mad Libs®

Sleepover Party Mad Libs®

Son of Mad Libs®

Sooper Dooper Mad Libs®

Spooky Mad Libs®

Straight "A" Mad Libs®

Totally Pink Mad Libs®

Undead Mad Libs®

Upside Down Mad Libs®

Vacation Fun Mad Libs®

We Wish You a Merry Mad Libs®

Winter Games Mad Libs®

You've Got Mad Libs®

and many, many more!
Mad Libs® are available wherever books are sold.